Sunflowers & Scars

Emily Marie Parker

BookLeaf
Publishing

India | USA | UK

Presentation by *BookLeaf Publishing*

Web: www.bookleafpub.com

E-mail: info@bookleafpub.com

ISBN: 9789358314649

First edition 2023

DEDICATION

First things first;

I'd like to thank my wonderful Mum for her constant support, guidance and encouragement. And more importantly - for always believing in me.

Witnessing her tackle and defeat every shitstorm that tried to destroy her while I was growing up made me the strong and ambitious woman that I am today.

Mum single-handedly helped instil all of the confidence and little ingredients needed to achieve all of my goals and to go ahead and publish this book.

I love you, always.

I'd also like to thank my all-time favourite human and therapist, Gem, for being the most hilarious, kind-hearted, gentle soul.

For embracing my quirks and for understanding me better than anyone else on the planet, even myself.

For being on constant stand-by whenever I'm hungover, anxious and feeling needy and for giving me all the reassurance needed to get me through the day. Thanks for being my number one fan and telling me that I'm good enough whenever I feel worthless. Without your friendship, adjusting to life back in England would have been a trillion times harder and I'm so blessed to have met you.

You really are one of life's angels.

Finally. I'd like to thank Roxanne - for being my rock over the years. For being there for me through thick and through thin. Our friendship has only strengthened as we've grown into adults.

We could go months without seeing each other but whenever I need you, I know you'll always be there in a heartbeat. Your family has always treated me like their own and for that I'll always be grateful. I just know that we'll be the best of friends until we're old and grey.

ACKNOWLEDGEMENT

This book is dedicated to my dog, Dottie.
(Unfortunately she can't read it.)

PREFACE

Emily is a 28-year-old poet from Blackburn, Lancashire, UK.

Jumping on a one-way flight to Southern China at just 20 years old meant she would chase her dreams of teaching English to children abroad. It was there where she fell in love with Chinese culture and quickly became fluent in Mandarin. . When the Covid-19 pandemic hit, due to visa issues this meant she had no choice but to pack up and leave the country in which she'd spent all of her adult life.

Struck with a terrible case of reverse culture shock Emily turned to poetry as a form of therapy whilst settling into a place that no longer felt like home. Emily wrote "Sunflowers & Scars" on some of her darkest days and through writing this book it helped her on the journey to finding herself.

Little Flower

Be strong; little flower
That's all that you can do
Don't give up now
Because, when today is through...

There will be a brand new day
full of hope and wonder
It's okay if today,
you need to stay under-

-That rock of darkness
and hide away from the world
To escape those
cruel words that were hurled.

But quickly! Get up now.
Before your roots get too dry
Chop chop, straighten up,
come on… Don't be shy!

Your delicate petals
They're withering one by one
And the heavy weight of regret
feels like ten tonne.

Stop beating yourself up
Shake yourself off and just breathe
you're in control now
you can stay or you can leave.

But; little flower, please remember…
To water yourself
Go outside, feel the sun
do it for your mental health.

Just like pollen, stick to those
who care about you
Go to the park, on a drive,
enjoy that nice view.

Because today might be gloomy
and you don't want to be here
But tomorrow might be glorious
and also next year…

Could be the best year of your life
You could grow ever so tall!
You could be a beautiful yellow sunflower
Climbing high against a wall.

Or a pretty white lily
full of innocence and purity
A red rose oozing romance
affection and security.

You could be that lotus
that grows on muddy, murky waters
Yet grows up to be kind
And inspire sons and daughters.

So… Little flower;

Don't give up.
Tomorrow's a new day
Things will get better
and everything will be okay.

Reverse Culture Shock

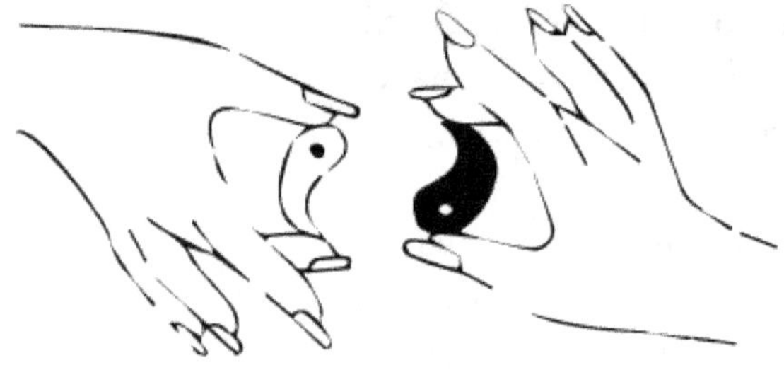

When you feel so alone
in the place you grew up
The changes you face
it's all so abrupt.

People in your hometown
They don't know all you've done
You were brave and adventured
They only know where it begun.

You've seen life

from a new point of view
you no longer judge
or feel the need to assume.

The poverty that you've witnessed
with your own very eyes
These fascinating experiences
how they make you grow wise.

The world is so big
so full of beauty and wonder
So climb, girl, climb
There's no need to stay under…

…That rock that's so safe
and so full of routine
Delve into the unknown
explore the unseen.

You only live once
so romanticise it all
Travel through Winter and Spring
and Summer and Fall.

Enjoy that cappuccino
all by yourself
Be grateful for your family
for your friends and your health.

Dive into valleys down low
climb mountains way up high
But what if I fall?
Oh but my darling, what if you fly?

Life is all about making
choices and decisions
Chase all your goals
and achieve your ambitions.

With hard work and dedication
you can do anything
engineering in Sydney
or teaching English in Beijing.

The options are endless
no need to follow a map
Fall in love with yourself
or with a hunky new chap.

Our lives are so different
So unique and so rare
But promise me one thing, Darling,
your stories, you must share.

Dark thoughts

She used to think
of those tall buildings
falling down
to end dark feelings.

Now she thinks
of boxes of pills
Wondering how
she'll pay these bills.

The battle in her mind
is so damn hard
All the pain she feels
it just won't discard.

The words she wants to say
people can't relate
Why? Oh, why?
Does she feel such hate....

The reflection of her

in the mirror
She simply just can't
recognise her.

A loving smile
an act of kindness
But behind closed doors
she's pure reckless.

The thoughts in her head
they swallow her up
That bottle of rum
She will 'sup.

All she wants is for
someone to care
Someone to listen
to stroke her hair.

She wants to think
the future's bright
She cries herself
to sleep at night.

She wants to make
them all feel proud
Instead she gets lost
in the crowd.

Amongst the many
likes and views
She ain't all that happy
where are the clues?

Does she laugh
and joke away?
Does she always have
a lot to say?

Does she decline
your invite for drinks?
Deeper and deeper
she slowly sinks…

Please do not judge
she means no harm
Just gently stroke her
on the arm.

Tell her that she matters
and it's all not true
when she says
she is a failure, too.

"Be kind" we say
but we don't preach
To our sons and daughters
a lesson we teach.

The King's meal

Society says that I belong to him
That I must give him what he craves
But my appetite; it is different
My hunger; it comes in waves.

I wish instead that he'd devour my soul
In this moment insecurities leave me full
But if I don't feed him now
He'll glaze me vanilla, bland and dull.

He stares at me with ravenous eyes
My rump he longs to taste
But inside I'm much more sweet
He lets that delicacy go to waste.

He's already grown al dente
But I am yet to boil
If I don't give him what he's ordered
Will he fail to remain loyal?

So naturally… I give in
I serve the King his meal
While he is feeling satisfied
Like a slab of meat I feel.

Insta-love

Twenty first-century love
Swiping left or right
Leaving me on read
Is bound to cause a fight.

If only this love was easy
No need to play such games
If we could measure passion
We'd combust into flames.

A heart-eyed emoji

Lets me know that you are keen
If only there weren't others
Who managed to get in-between.

A green icon shows you're chatting
But it is not with me
I have a fifties loyal heart
If only you could see.

I dream that we'd go dancing
Or see a black-and-white flick
I wouldn't need to worry
about any other chick.

Instagram, Snapchat
and an Only-Fans
What ever happened to
simply holding hands...

Walking a girl home at night
innocent pecks on the cheek
Hoping that you'd see her again
the very next week.

Am I cat fishing?
I wish I could be thin.
Is there competition?
May the best avatar win.

Two-hundred and thirty likes
On the selfie she's just posted
"And it's only been 10 minutes"
She so confidently boasted.

But fuck your beauty standards
I'd rather just be real
For I am more than worthy
And to the right one I will appeal.

Open minds

Do you ever feel
like you just don't belong?
only way to express yourself
is to post lyrics to that song.

You feel like they're laughing at you
for not being just like them
Am I weird? Am I strange?
My opinions; they just seem to condemn.

Over there, you look different
Your complexion is not the same
Your eyes a peculiar green
And they make fun of your frame.

Back here, you can't relate
to what they're all gossiping about
When you mention that time in Vietnam
They interrupt; with a selfie and a pout.

The fact is, our lives
are all so beautifully unique
So ignore those silly comments
who are they to critique?

Dan might move to Africa
to give aid to those in need
And Jane might be a stay-at-home Mum
with plenty of mouths to feed.

Lucy might not want children,
She wants to focus on her career
And Ben; he wants to go travelling
And make the most of his gap year.

Be kind to one another
You don't know what battles they might face
Compliment, empower and love
No matter what gender, age or race.

To be truly open-minded
is a wonderful trait to possess
To see the world from your eyes
Will only lead to success.

Bonfire heart

Violent bursts of ivory
emerald and scarlet red
fields flooded with Fawkes
all gazing ahead.

Tonight love fills the air
your family joins mine
children prancing happily
way after nine.

She's never looked as elegant

as the way she does right now
her delicate face devoured by the sky
steals away my heart, somehow.

Flames fierce and fragrant
smiling faces galore
sons sat on shoulders
this atmosphere, I adore.

But did you ever wonder?
Why fireworks never showcase blue?
for years pyrotechnicians
have been trying to produce this colour, too.

But it is just impossible
As is trying to end my love for you.
But one thing is for sure,
Without you…
Lord knows, I'm feeling blue.

Life on the spectrum

Some may say that I'm different
But in fact I'm unique
My eyes speak many a word
When my voice fails to speak.

To live in my world
Is a lot different than yours
The most trivial of tasks
To me is the biggest of chores.

Damn you - mess on my hands!
I just want to stay clean!!!
I like things in order
I'm a huge fan of routine.

Butter on my toast?
But I like to eat it dry!
My world's crumbling around me
All I can do is cry.

Sometimes I struggle
Sometimes I stutter
Watching things fall to the ground
Makes my heart flutter.

I'm in love with numbers
Some say that I'm gifted
To put things in order
What a weight lifted!

My friends all play together
While I play in the corner on my own
But please; don't be fooled
For I am not alone.

I like it this way
Exploring this vibrant world around me
So let me spread my wings
Allow me to be free.

But please understand;
When I'm covering my ears
Loud sounds and bright lights
Are some of my biggest fears.

I'm a sensitive soul
In so many ways
So please remember that
When I'm stood in a daze.

I'll send you a virtual hug
As I'm not keen on touch
Sometimes it's difficult to show
But I love you ever so much.

Beer fear

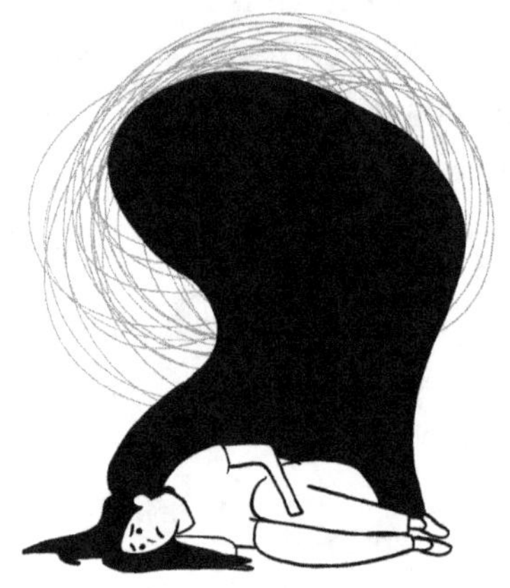

Beer fear
Beer fear
Positive reassurance
I need to hear.

Hangxiety level;
369
Why did I drink
my body weight in wine?

Does everyone hate me?
Am I a bad person?
All these awful thoughts
Just seem to worsen.

What is my life?
I'm such a mess
Could you see my knickers
Through my dress?

Jäger bombs
Sambuca shots
How many rounds?
Fucking lots.

Why did I say that?
I showed myself up
Why didn't I eat?
Boy did I 'sup!

My camera roll
I daren't look
Why am I such
A silly fuck?

You've been tagged in a video
Oh kill me now!
Silly Billy awards...
Please take a bow.

Googling can you die
From a hangover?
Munching on last night's
Leftovers.

No more drinking
Let's reign it in
My head is a jungle
Put myself in the bin.

Remember that tomorrow:
Your mind will be clean
To yourself;
Stop being so mean!

You had a great night
Your makeup was on fleek
You might be dying now but….
Same time next week?

Narcissist

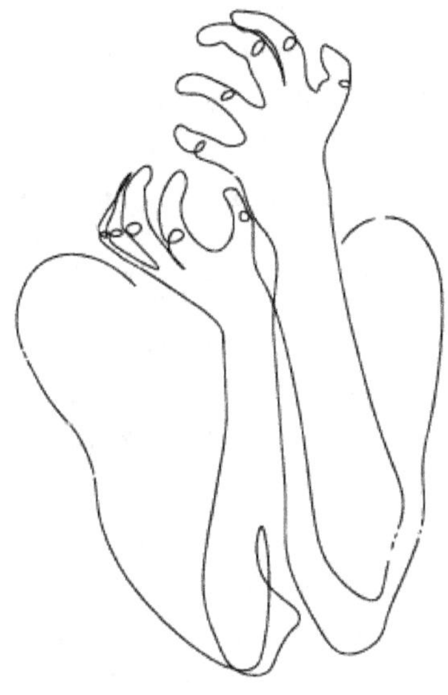

He'll bounce into your life
Saying things you've always wanted to hear
You'll feel like you've won the lottery
He'll always want to keep you near.

He'll buy your favourite flowers
Make sure to open the car door
But little do you know, sweetheart;
He's always keeping score.

While the love-bombing commences

Do not tell him of your fears
For he will use these insecurities
As ammunition through the years.

Don't tell him how you hate your nose
How you're repulsed by your stretch marks
At the time his ear feels safe to tell
But will soon be used as nasty remarks.

He'll manipulate conversations
Have you doubting what you said
You prefer to communicate via text
To be sure that you've not misread…

-The words he likes twist and turn
To put the blame back onto you
When he is caught and feels threatened
He'll bring 2012 up out of the blue.

Once he was the light of your life
Now all he does is gas-light
Questions circle round your mind
Keeping you up throughout the night.

The constant lying and betrayal
His inflated ego overpowers
He'll have you questioning your sanity
Sobbing hysterically for hours.

The constant highs and lows
Have you craving this addiction
But I'm sorry to burst your bubble, Darling;
this love story is pure fiction.

So get rid of your narcissist
Erase him from your heart
Right now things might seem blue
But things will get better once you part.

The drug

Constantly feeling
the need to compare
Beating myself up
for not being like her.

I bet she's not awkward
bet she doesn't forget what to say
I bet he's thinking of her
In this bed where we lay.

She's the one who he craves
The one who lives in his mind
Wishing it was her hair grips
Around his house he would find.

She's glowing and radiant
I'm crippled with flaws
I've been hurt in the past
And it's apparent, it shows.

I blend into the background
Confidence oozes from her skin
While she's in the picture
His heart - I'll never win.

How could I ever compare?
He's addicted to her taste
While he's hooked on that drug
My love goes to waste.

But that drug will destroy him
Believe me I've been there myself
I hope he can end this addiction
For his own mental health.

R.I.P baby Jacob

TW - child abuse

I'm one month old
Full of gummy smiles
Mummy's soothing voice
I can hear it for miles.

She's taking a video of me
Is it because I'm so cute?
Daddy doesn't like when I cry
I'll try my best to be mute.

But sometimes I'm hungry
My tummy is so sore
I tremble when Daddy
Comes crashing through the door.

Sometimes I want a cuddle
I want to feel my skin on theirs
So all I can do is cry
Oh no! They're marching up the stairs.

Sometimes Daddy makes jokes
Jokes about me being dead.
But of course he's only joking…
Daddy's such a silly head.

I think Daddy will like me
When I'm all grown up
When I'm all clean and smart
And not such a mucky pup.

I've got the same name as Daddy
Jacob. Craig. Crouch.
But why does he keep hurting me?
My ribs bruised. Ouch.

I don't think Mummy
likes me either; anymore.
She laughs and smiles when
Daddy makes my body all sore.

I remember when I was tiny
When I was cute and sweet
Mummy used to give me

Nice things to eat.

That last punch Daddy gave me
Was much harder than the rest
Maybe it was my fault
For being such a pest.

But this ouchy is different
I think Daddy broke my bone
I wish someone would cuddle me
I'm in this cot all alone.

I'm sorry Mummy and Daddy
For not making you proud
Maybe I would still be here
If I didn't cry so loud.

I hear that in heaven
There're lots of children just like me
I can't wait to meet them
Pelka, Star Hobson and baby P.

They say that us little angels
Are too good for this Earth
So in heaven we'll dance together
And we'll forever know our worth.

Be kind

Be kind to Liam
'Cause he's feeling low
The last time he truly laughed
Feels like a life-time ago.

Tell Lily she looks lovely
In that little black dress
The reflection in the mirror
Causes her so much distress.

Don't forget to invite Emma
Just because she's expecting
Don't make her stay at home
Overthinking and reflecting.

Bitchin' 'bout Beth
Ain't gonna make you any better
She could really help your business
If only you would let her.

Be a shoulder to cry on
Listen to Rachel rant
Be sensitive to her problems
Become an agony aunt.

Lend Chris a cheeky tenner
Till his payday next week
He's in debt up to his eyeballs
Asking for help makes him feel weak.

Tell Dom that he's a cracking Dad
He simply is the best.
To have a man like him around
His kids are truly blessed.

Smile at that stranger
walking down the road
Changing their outlook on life
With the kindness that you showed.

Hibernate

She wished that she could curl up
Into a little ball
Close her eyes, rest her bones.
Breathe…..
But most of all…

Wake up with a fresh new mind
All her worries - erased.
She longs for those old times
When she was barely phased.

Hibernate all through the Winter
All of her energy she would save.
Protect herself from the cold
Positive words she would engrave…

Into her mind…
So, when she finally wakes
She'll remember how to love herself
Despite her many mistakes.

Absent Father

That little girl
without her dad

at the time
she didn't know she was sad.

For she hadn't known
any other way
Her Mother always knew
just what to say.

Her stepdad was perfect
how she wished he was hers
he was kind and caring
and taught her to share.

Although he was loving
it just wasn't the same
when in-fact
she didn't share his last name.

Where does she come from?
Does she look like her "Dad"?
The thought of him leaving
makes her feel mad.

How could he not want to be a
part of his daughter's life?
To see her succeed
To one day become a wife.

She used to think without him

she'd be fine
Who'd have known that
later down the line…

She'd feel so upset
betrayed and hurt
with older men;
she would flirt.

But in fact she wants
to find the right guy
Who won't hurt her
and make her cry.

Just like you have done
so many times
To be an absent father
should be a crime.

Why did you leave?
Was it all her fault?
The wounds you caused
are filled with salt.

When one day
you suddenly appear…
For twenty-six years
you've been nowhere near.

Well I'm sorry dear "Father"
you had your chance
To love your daughter
with all you had.

But you chose
to stay away
her life she lived
everyday.

Without your love
she still survived
She moved abroad
oh how she thrived!

You don't deserve
to know her now…
My absent father…
Please take a bow.

M.O.T your kids.

Oh, you want to drive a car?
Plenty of lessons - you must book
You want to raise a baby?
Here you are - good luck!

God forbid you drive a car
Until you've passed both exams
But how to operate a baby?
Oh, just stick it in a pram.

I believe to become a parent
A mandatory course should be completed
To ensure you know what it entails
So that history isn't repeated.

Your trusty little Corsa
Sure to have an M.O.T every year
But your 16-year-old daughter
A health professional's been nowhere near.

Her headlights are fading dimmer
Her engine is running slow
She's got scrapes on her exterior
But little did you know…
Her breaks don't squeak when they're broken
She isn't stopped if a light is out

She parks alone in her bedroom.
If she is loved she often doubts.

She compares herself to that Audi
Worries her boot is too wide
So give her an M.O.T
Be the one in which she can confide.

All you need to do is listen
Make sure that you are there
Give her an M.O.T
Just let her know you care.

Monster Daddy

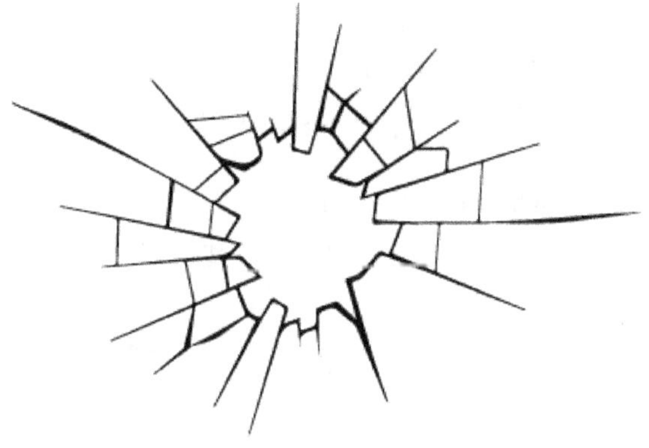

She's trying her best to be a Mother
But she's a much better punching bag
While she's trying to feed the baby
She's spat at and called a "slag".

She believes that he will change
Maybe he's got the baby blues
She's still blinded by that first year love
His obscenities; she'll excuse.

The vulgar ways which he describes her

Stick so strongly in her mind
Yet in them; she's trying to instil
confidence
and the importance of being kind.

But Daddy is far from kind to Mummy
He's as evil as they come.
Now Mummy suffers from PTSD
From his punches; she's grown numb.

She knows that she can't leave
The girls need both their Mum and Dad
She doesn't want her babies
To have the same experiences she's had.
She grew up without a father
She's adamant that history shan't repeat.
So she stays with their monster Daddy.
She allows herself to be beat.

"But he's so good with the girls"
"He'd never lay a finger on them"
Still Monster Daddy lives amongst them
Even after the Social strongly condemn.

What she doesn't realise now;
Staying will cause her daughters far more
damage
Watching their Mummy beaten to a pulp.
Their sweet Daddy is a savage.

But this hospital trip is different.
Mummy won't leave with bandages and slings.
This time; Monster Daddy
Caused Mummy to gain her angel wings.

Tommy

Just three weeks on Earth
How he craves skin-on-skin
Colic cries erupt from
the crib he's dumped in.

"Just leave him to cry"
"He'll soon get fed up"
As they turn up the music
Stella cans they will 'sup.

Tommy turns up to nursery

With a cut on his face
His nappy full to the brim
His clothes a disgrace.

At four years of age
He's never known love
He's familiar with rage
How to push, how to shove.

"Last night Daddy hurt Mummy
And that made me cry…
Now Mummy's lip is bigger
She's got black on her eye."

The nice lady at the nursery
on her knee he would sit
While Mum sits in an alley
Consumed by that hit.

When snack time comes
He's the first one in line
Fighting over broken crackers
"Get off! That's mine!"

"Stop that crying or I'll give
You something to cry for"
His teachers are daft
If they believe he walked into a door.

Tommy's thirty now
How to love; he does not know
The only relationship he has
Is his relationship with blow.

"Useless" "good for nothing"
And "little shit"
Are just a few of the comments
That just seem to stick-

In his broken mind
So lost and so confused
On the streets he sleeps now
A hostel; he was refused.
Blow turns to brown
As he struggles mentally to cope
He's found alone in that alley
Tommy's overdosed on dope.

That same alley
Where his mother had her first hit.
His tormented childhood
caused little Tommy to commit.

Dan's Debt

Dan was a simple man
never into drink or drugs
He never really showed his emotions
He wasn't a huge fan of hugs.

Dan was one of the good ones
He wasn't a materialistic guy
Dan kept himself to himself
Never would he harm a fly.

Dan did the same thing

Almost every single day
He'd walk his Labrador through the park
He'd even walk the same way.

That was until he met Grace
His saving Grace (cliche I know)
After meeting that girl
A spring in his step began to show.

Dan wasn't used to love
As a kid; he'd never been shown
This new love he had acquired
Made Dan request a payday loan.

Dan wanted to make his Grace
feel some special kind of way
Even if it meant in-instalments
Was the only way to pay.

He'd buy her everything she'd dreamed of
Jewellery and handbags galore
She was the light of his world
He loved her to the very core.

Dan got a loan to pay a loan
Then one more to pay one more
Without a doubt; each one
Tainting his credit rating score:

Before Dan knew it
Debt collectors were at his door
They'd taken Grace's engagement ring
She'd kept it safe in their top drawer.

Through the stress and the worry
Dan turned to drink
They were about to lose the house
Deeper and deeper he would sink.

Grace got fed up
This wasn't the life she had planned
Dan hadn't a pot to piss in
And in debt by thirty grand.

When Dan received that blow
His life; how it shattered
His darling soul mate, Grace
She was the only thing that mattered.

Grace returned to collect her stuff
But she wouldn't stop to wave
Little did she know in the back bedroom;
Debt had taken Dan to the grave.

Find yourself

When you're lost in a vast world
Neither meek nor mild
Searching for that inner peace
To match the smile she smiled.

Ask yourself; Who really am I?
Do you even have a clue?
Should the answer be no; then off you go
To discover what makes you, you.

Explore what makes your heart sing
And all that makes you tick
How did you become who you are today?
Through common sense or logic?

Study your love language
Question your spirituality
Find out your darkest fears
And why they cause you anxiety.

Understand what you need
And more importantly; what you don't
Don't ever let cruelty warp you
Your kindness; you must flaunt.

Embrace your emotions
Never keep them trapped within
Listen to your body
Be comfortable in your own skin.

Allow yourself to heal
Cleanse those wounds and scars
Without this all-important step
You'll never see the stars.

Once you're certain of who you are
Self-love will devour your soul
Lacking a lover will never be lonesome
Because you yourself; are whole.

Some Days

Some days are harder
Some days are rough
Some days you wonder
If you are enough.

Some days are confusion
Some days just aren't clear
Some days are full of
anxiety and fear.

Some days you regret

Some days you look back
Some days you feel as though
You're just not on track.

Some days are numb
Some days you cry
Some days you've no energy
To get up and try.

Some days you're alone
Trapped inside your own mind
Some days to yourself
You're anything but kind.

But some days are sparkles
Some days are glitter
Some days you remind yourself
That you're not a quitter.

Some days are sunflowers
Some days are laughter
Some days are everything
You've always been after.

Some days are blue.
But some days are bright
Some days aren't perfect
But that's alright.

Broken best friend.

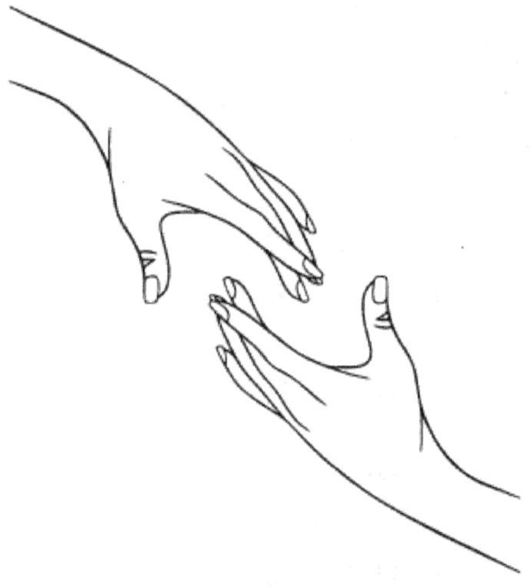

She doesn't realise her beauty,
she doesn't know her worth
She politely denies the flattery
She's the sweetest thing on Earth.

She's sunshine on a Summer's day
She's witty banter when you're down
She's the one to pick you up
When all you want to do is frown.

It's criminal, the things she's been through

How she's been so unlucky in love
How they've made her feel about herself Yet she
still puts everyone above-

Herself, Because her heart is pure Her soul is
one of a kind
Despite all the pain she's felt
She always keeps others in mind.

She's sensitive and passionate
A true Aquarian indeed
She always gives her all
She always strives to succeed.

She's a powerful, fiery lioness
Her two cubs are her whole life
With her around they'll see no harm
For them, she'd take a knife.

She doubts her every being
When others pray to be like her
She's blind to her reflection
In the mirror, she's a blur.

She's a bright and vibrant sunflower
She's a picnic in the park
It breaks my heart to see her hurt
How can I pull her from the dark?

When you've lived abroad

You value village venues
When you've lived abroad
You long for local accents
The better the more broad.

When you've lived abroad
You lap up all that green
Our British countrysides
Breathtakingly serene.

You relish in roast dinners
When you've lived away
You ache for afternoon tea
Apologies if it is cliche.

You crave Coronation Street
When you've lived overseas
You search for some sarcasm
You long to be teased.

When you've lived abroad
You yearn for a Yorkshire pud
You'd give anything for gravy
Even your left arm if you could.

You prefer Fridays with the family
When you've lived the life of an Ex-Pat
You live for the little things
Like those lovely little chats.

When you've lived far away
You treasure water from the tap
You can walk almost anywhere
No need to take a map.

Living away all those years
How it opened up my eyes.
I don't regret a single second.
Each moment made me grow wise.

But returning back home
I've fallen in love with myself
I'm thankful for my family
For my friends and my health.

Because of you

Because of you:
I fear they're all the same
My reflection in the mirror
fills me with shame.

Because of you:
I doubt their compliment is real.
I refuse to feel the emotions
that they want me to feel.

Because of you:
self-sabotage is the safest way
I refuse to be an opponent
in the potential games they play.

Because of you:
green flags all have a hint of red
All those warped little words
linger in my head.

Because of you:
my heart no longer sits on my sleeve
At any sign of danger
I want to run and leave.

Because of you:
memories manipulate my every day
Waiting for the day
that they inevitably stray.

Because of you:
my walls are made strong of pure graphene
Because of you:
I may lose the brightest flag of green.

Him

She saw something in him
Something that no one else did
She delved into the depths of his darkness
The parts of him he preferred were hid.

She embraced each flaw
Each insecurity she'd devour
She saw the sweetness in him
The segments others saw as sour.

She refused to believe
To believe that he in fact was dirt
If it's true what others said
It's because deep inside he's hurt.

She saw the light within him

That glimmer of hope she held onto
Never would she tarnish his name
She saw him from a different point of view.

Don't do it

Pondering all the methods
By noose. To jump. Or pop pills...
Mental health; it is ruthless.
Sadly; depression kills.

Don't listen to those voices
Telling you to just quit
My ear is always open
Next to me, please sit...

Don't do it. I beg.
You are worthy. Please know.
The world will be much darker
If you decide you have to go.

A Mother will be childless
A dog will lose it's world
Devastation will erupt
To each loved one - unfurled.

Your Mam; riddled with regret
Asking "was it all my fault?"
Absent Mother's Day cards
Each year will fill her wounds with salt.

Your childhood best friend
Full of anguish and torment
Constantly replaying all the good times
Together you both spent.

The world won't be better off
A burden; you are not.
Despite what you may think
Never could you be forgot.

Remember that girl from school?
The one which you always held a flame?
She was hoping you'd ask her out
Today she fills herself with blame.

Bob from the corner shop
Will be devastated by the news
How he loved to wind you up
When to Burnley; Rovers would lose.

A huge Facebook tribute
Blue and white hearts will be shared
An abundance of crying emojis
From all the folk that cared.

So don't do it. I beg.
You are worthy. Please know.
The world is a brighter place with you in it
And many people love you so.

Do you want children?

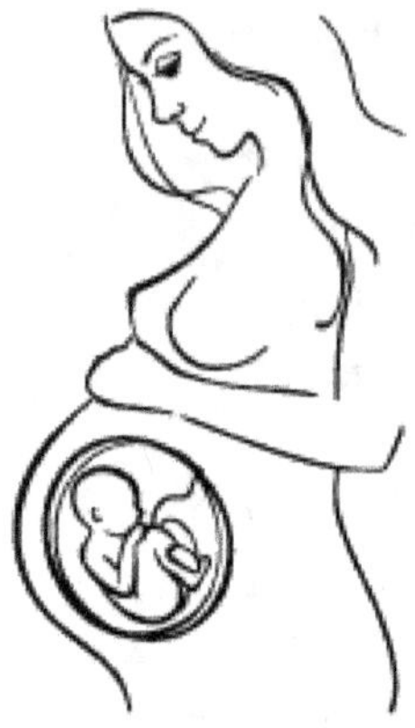

"Do you want children?"
A question so profound
The question has only gotten more difficult
As I've gotten older I have found.

Ever since I was a little girl
It had always been my dream
Kids dangling from both legs
I wanted my own football team.

I had always been maternal
I wanted nothing more from life
I'd protect them at any cost
For my babies; I'd take a knife.

But what if I cannot protect?
From this world that's so corrupt
Or what if my dear child
Heads down a path of self-destruct?

What if my child gets ill
The kind of ill that starts with "C"
And I can't take away her pain
I can't transfer it onto me.

What if one day life gets too much
And I decide that I must leave
That option is erased
When you've got little mouths to feed.

What if for just one moment
For just a second; she feels unloved
What if while Mummy's not there
In the playground; she is shoved.

What if at Christmas time
Her friend's presents are way more
What if; God forbid
There happens to be a third world war?

What if her Daddy leaves?
And she decides she's not enough?
What if I'm having a bad day

And on my daughter I'm too tough.

What if her first love
Leaves her heart broken and shattered
Or she's a victim of DV
Left on the floor bruised and battered.

What if she's minding her own business
Just walking down the street
And in a cruel twist of fate
A sadistic killer she will meet.
And despite all of these worries
The endless anxiety and stress
Ask me "Do you want children?"
The answer will be "yes".

Poetic embassy

You let me feel my big feelings without
judgement
Oh, how very fluid you are
You listen to my thoughts
The morbid, the outrageous and the bizarre.

You are my refuge
To you; I'll always run
Each word speaks to my soul
Every stanza and every pun.

When the sun's no longer shining
And it feels like nothing's going right
In you; I shall confide
I'll pick up a pen and I will write.

You are my poetic embassy
Sheltering me from the dark
Wherever I go I'll take you with me
Etched on my skin like a birthmark.

Dottie

Black, white and chocolate brown
The colours of her fur
Inquisitive head turns, curious grunts
When she hears the bowl I stir.

Some may say "But it's just a dog"
In fact, that's just not the case
Some days I feel I wouldn't be here
If it wasn't for her embrace.

She feels when I'm not cheery
On my knee she rests her paw
Her charming eyes look up at me
The loveliest specimen I ever saw.

She greets me with an animated cry
Her fluffy tail dances with glee
I'm viciously attacked with kisses
Only three minutes passed since she's seen me.

Although she does not talk like you and I
Her eyes speak many a word
To her, I narrate my every thought
Again, some may say "that's absurd."

Once, I had to live my life alone
Without her by my side
While I was here and she was there
No one I had in to confide.

Those long eight months were crippling
Every night, my pillow soaked-
With tears for my dog, so far away...
By strangers; she was stroked.

Where she belongs, she has returned
Curled right upon my knee
It is my promise from this day on
never again, will she part from me.

A book

A book is a safe place
Somewhere to hide.
A book is an adventure
An emotional ride.

A book makes you feel
Makes you think outside the box
A book teaches morals
Sometimes portrayed by a fox.

A book is magic
A whole new realm
A sudden twist of events
Can at times overwhelm.

A book is food
Food for the brain
A book soothes your mind
When you feel you're going insane.

A book is a councillor
From a crippling reality
A book is a language
A different kind of mentality.

A book is addiction
When I need a fix
Devouring pages
All three hundred and six.

A book is a compass
Directing us in different ways
A book feeds us knowledge
To help with our essays.

So come on, don't be shy
Go to the library for a peek
Pick up yourself a thriller
If it's suspense that you seek.

To dive into a book
is never too late
Who knows what exciting
escapades await?

February

Oh February...
You are the month of affection
Mother of Aquarians and Pisceans
You made us both to perfection.

.

The second month gave us Shakira
The one whose hips don't lie
Queens are born in February
That you can't deny.

The only month that thought "fuck this!!"

As they got towards the end...
"Well, how about every 4 years?"
The other 11 months recommend...

Thanks for allowing our mate;
Ed Sheeran
To think out loud
If you were born in February
You should be ever so proud.

Ronaldo, Rihanna
and Harry Styles
Kurt Cobain, Johnny Cash;
the list goes on for miles.........
Many a legend was born;
in the month of Amethyst
And that's not including
the ones that we have missed.

In The English language;
one of the most misspelt words...
We're sorry for the confusion
But most of us are nerds.

Anyway the aim of this poem;
Is to make you realise
That February is the elite month
Apologies if I patronise.

Netflix and chill

She's always there for you and I
Oh how she gets turned on
Controlled by many a man
Women sobbing at "Dear John."

We pay for her services
Unless you tag team with your mate
Just don't be tempted to rely on her
When you're only on your second date.

Romance makes us hopeful
Horrors; they make us jump
Comedies cheer us up
When the guy we like gave us the hump.

Sometimes she makes us howl
She makes our stomach hurt
Other times we are disgusted
Glued to true crimes on a pervert.

She force-fed us Jeffery Dahmer
Wednesday; we had to watch
Tinder Swindler giving men ideas
Women worship Magic Mike's crotch.

She offers all kinds of stand-up
Lazy days when it's not sunny
Some may not understand her humour
"That's not even remotely funny."

Thank you Dear Netflix
For allowing us to "chill"
Life wouldn't be the same without you
But please, do not increase your bill.

Eat or Heat

"It's like Blackpool
illuminations in here"
A saying; we no longer hear.
For to turn on a light; we all fear.

2022, Oh what a year.
"I'm freezing Mum"
"Go and get a quilt"
No parent should have
to feel this guilt.

To turn on the heating
Or buy a meal
These difficult times;
we all feel.

It's Brian; who I think
about the most
He can't afford his
marmalade on toast.

For seventy years
His morning routine
Grafted his ass off
Since he was fifteen

Now he's retired
It's his time to rest
Under his pyjamas
Lies a thermal vest.

He fought for our country
He did us all proud
Now he sits at home
Teeth chattering ever so loud.

In these hard times
We must stick together
It's easier said than done
Not to lose our tether.

One thing is for sure
We're all in the same boat
Come round mine for a brew
But don't forget your big coat.

Your person

If they are your person
you won't have any doubt
You'll finally be at peace
Won't feel the need to shout.

They won't try to test you.
Your buttons, they won't push.
They won't try to make you jealous
They won't keep you on the hush.

They'd pick you out

Of a busy crowd
Their actions
Would speak so loud.

They'd choose you
Every single day
Never would they leave
They'd always stay.

They'd put you high upon
A pedestal
Their love for you
Known to all.

From rooftops,
They'd roar your name
Their love for you
They would proclaim.

They'd be your person
And you'd be theirs
No one would come close
No other compares.

Pisces

She is fiercely independent
Dances to the beat of her own drum
She wants you. Doesn't need you.
She will not live under any thumb.

Words of affirmation;
Her chosen love language
If you speak to her soul
You'll be heading for marriage.

She loves like there is no tomorrow
Forgives like there's no yesterday
Forgives but doesn't forget, however,
The times you lead her astray.

Her kindness often mistaken for weakness
In that case, you don't know her well
Must you cross her loved ones
She'll kindly drag you to hell.

Ruled by Neptune
She's creative, wise and dreamy
Effortlessly adaptable
Between the sheets, hot and steamy.

Mysterious and intuitive
She relies on her sixth sense
To protect herself and her dearest
Some may say she's intense.

She's charming and poetic
In her own world she lives
She's gentle and generous
Her last penny, she gives.

She is Pisces.
She wears her heart on her sleeve.
Sometimes misunderstood
Sometimes difficult to perceive.

Lucky.

How lucky I am
To breathe in and out
How lucky I am
To just walk about.

That time I was injured
and I couldn't stand
Made me realise
That actually, my life is grand.

I'm grateful for hot chocolate

In my favourite mug
I appreciate medicine
When I catch a bug.

Baths filled with bubbles
Are what I live for
These everyday things
We all should adore.

Sunflowers, bees
And all things yellow
All capture my heart
They make me feel mellow.

Thankful for books
When I'm feeling stressed
expression through poetry
Makes me feel blessed.

I'm grateful for porridge
For coffee and tea
In some countries
These things, you can't guarantee.

These little details
are taken for granted
"I want that new iPhone!"
He selfishly ranted.

Value time with friends
Or time on my own
Writing poems on the bus
When I'm in the zone.

These early mornings
how I am in awe
I fall in love with
the most charming meadow.

Positive affirmations
Tell yourself day-to-day
Believe everything is exciting
Even the most mundane.
For this is when
We become truly alive
Life is for living
Not only to survive.

Warrior

She puts on a brave face
seven days a week
When inside she's slowly crumbling
Medical attention; she must seek.

She's a warrior.

She's drained, both physically and mentally
How much more of this can she take?
But still the show must go on...
Resilience won't allow her to break.

She's a warrior.

Despite her many battles
She's the perfect wife-to-be
She created two lovely miracles
They're both her down to a T!

She's a warrior.

One princess and one prince
They're so lucky to have her near
When she looks into their smiling eyes
Her inner-demons disappear.

She's a warrior.

Excruciating pain
leaves her self-conscious, weak and tearful
Yet she still drags herself into work
With a pretty smile, acting cheerful.

She's a warrior.

Endometriosis is a big part of her life
But define her, it does not.
She's kind, caring, strong-minded and smart
I hope she knows, I care, a lot.

You can do this Uni motivation.

You've got this.
Vygotsky; you'll get used to hearing his name
He and Piaget are similar
but not quite the same.

He believed in development
culture plays a big part
But Piaget believes in stages
That children must begin at the start.

Well you've made your start
And for that you should be proud
Once you've completed your degree
You'll stand out from the crowd.

Don't worry... You'll soon know
your way around Moodle
Many of your evening meals
Will be a Bombay Bad Boy pot noodle.

And all of these theorists
they'll soon become your best mates
(After their name don't forget
To put in brackets the dates.)
Skinner and Bowlby
Bruner and Craft
Always remember
to submit your draft.

I never did...
and boy I was stressed!
Panicking the night before
Sends your head West.

Maslow's your guy
And his hierarchy of needs
Another word of advise
Log out from any social media feeds.

Don't fall down that rabbit hole
Just one more reel!
Overdosing on caffeine
Is also not ideal.

At the time; 6 cups of coffee
Seemed like such a good idea
I became the Duracell bunny
With a bad bout of diarrhoea.

Montessori and Froebel
Ainsworth and Freud
Are some of the names
That you just can't avoid.
If you can't get to class
Check the lessons that you've missed
And for crying out loud
Save your reference list.

Memes; they are funny
But they won't get you a degree
After all your hard work
Soon you'll be free.

Use more journals than sites
Wikipedia ain't your friend
And using an AI chatbot
I don't recommend.

Soon you'll be asked
your pedagogical approach
You certainly won't regret
Meeting the academic coach.

She'll help get you organised
If you're just like me
With your head in the clouds
And don't know your ass from your knee.

Remember to praise yourself
Just maybe not after every single line.
Well done! you've done 20 words
You deserve another glass of wine.
Oh and just one more thing!
Always believe in yourself
Take time to breathe
Take care of your mental health.

Because you are amazing
And your future looks bright
Now chop chop! Get a move on
You've got essays to write.

Secret Santa

Secret Santa
Secret Santa
Last minute mad rush
Down to Asda.

Candles for Carol
Some socks for Steve
Grab 7 Linx Africa
Everybody's pet peeve.

What gift to choose?

For my boss
Festive anal beads
Might make her cross.

For your favourite bro
A mug with the word "cunt"
Or an apron for your Nan
With a willy on the front.

Elfis the Elf
That little twat
Poured "reindeer food"
In my hat.

Down the baileys
Guzzle eggnog
Call your cousin a slag.
Grab your neighbour for a snog.

I asked Santa nicely
For a new pair of Docs
Must've been a naughty girl
'Cause he brought fucking Crocs.

New Year New Me

Soon will be that time of year
Standard "new year new me" posts
When you promise to join the gym
After all those scrummy roasts.

But you know that's a big fat lie
You're gonna stay the same old you.
The diet starts again on Monday
Erm... Joe Wicks who?!

Did somebody say Just Eat?
Quickly! Remove the app.
We don't want to get to April
Still being a silly fat wap.

'Cause then you'll be the April fool
Not sticking to their goals
Comparing to that Instagram model
Don't be tempted to 2 more bowls.

December is for noshing
And no, I don't mean that kind!
It's for inhaling celebrations by the box
No matter the size of your behind.

How many pigs in blankets
Can you cram into your gob?
I've discovered a new talent
I'm considering getting a new job.

The type of job that entails
Selling farts live on web-cam
The views would be rolling in
After brussels sprouts and glazed ham.

Or I'd smear myself in cranberry sauce
Upload it to only-fans
Because dieting is far too hard
That's definitely off the plans.

No So fuck "new year new me"
Stick to the angel you know.
As you are wonderfully unique.
And plenty of people love you so.

Bed Day

Today is a bed day
And in my bed is where I'll stay
It's the only place that I feel safe
So in my bed; I will lay.

I'm far too ugly to walk the streets
People shouldn't have to see this mug
I can't bear the thought of socialising
So I'll tell my friend I have a bug.

I don't want to travel to the living-room

It's much too bright out there
Today is a bed day.
And into thin air, I will stare.

I ask myself; do I really feel safe?
Or am I trapped within this bed?
Or even more importantly
Am I trapped in my own head?

Outside the world is laughing
I can hear them from this bed
I don't deserve to laugh
So I'll leave my friends on read.

Someone's knocking on my door
But they can't; I'm having a bed day
I'm not going to answer the door
They're just going to have to go away.

I wish this bed day would hurry up
It's taking so long to pass
While I am rotting in this bed
My mind continues to harass.

Sometimes bed days become bed weekends
Or even full-blown bed weeks
Is your friend having too many bed days?
Recognise the volumes that it speaks.

Coming out

At 27 years old I suddenly realised
Why things had been the way they were
Why I became nervous around them
At certain females; I would stare.

Looking back when I was 10 years young;
I thought I loved my TA.
I cried myself to sleep that night.
I didn't want to be this way

Seventeen years passed
With many men it didn't work
I needed more intensity
I'd been through many a jerk.

How did it never occur?
That I was wildly attracted to the X
I mean, we are the ultimate chromosome
Together; we make the best sex.

No offence to the Y's,
Sometimes I like you, too.
But unsolicited dick pics.
Boy, they make me spew.

Today; I feel so grateful
For opening that rainbow door
Intense emotion now reciprocated
Oh there's so much to explore.

I can relate to that saying; When they say "love
is love"
I'm proud to have found myself
And realise that I am enough.

Dear Santa

I'm writing you this letter
Because Today's December first
I know I'm not the best boy
But I don't think I'm the worst.

I always turn on my listening ears
And I promise I'm never mean
Last year I was good all year long
But maybe you just never seen.

Because you never came to my house
I really thought you would
I tried my hardest every single day
To be extra special good.

I woke up super early
To see if you had been
Why didn't you come Santa?
Is it because our house isn't clean?

Sometimes it smells funny in our house
I'll help my Mummy to clean up
I don't think we have any milk
So I'll leave a can for you to sup.

Mummy's boyfriend has lots of cans
And he has a fat tummy just like you
When I told him about your letter
He told me that Santa ain't true.

It's okay though, Santa
I don't want lots and lots and lots
Just a little small present is enough
Maybe a new pair of socks.

And pretty pretty please
Can I have just one more thing
A cuddly unicorn for my little sister
One of them ones that can sing.

Last week she lost her favourite teddy
So every day she's been so sad
We don't want anything fancy
Not a bike or an iPad.

Charlie and Oscar have an elf at home
He got delivered in a box
He does lots of silly things
He even poured cereal into their blocks!

Some children went on the bus today
While we were doing circle time
They got special tickets to see
A Christmas pantomime.

All my friends wore Christmas jumpers
But Mummy doesn't have pennies for that
And when we play outside
Mrs Blake lets me borrow a spare hat.

Mrs Blake bought me a chocolate calendar
She said it's specially for me
She lets me open every door
But not to let the other children see.

She says I'm such a good boy
She says I've got a heart of gold
I heard her say to Mr Jacobs
That she worries about me being cold.

So I really hope you'll come this year
Please don't forget about me
You can put my present under the stairs
Cos we don't have a Christmas tree.

I love you so much Santa
I hope you get this letter
And don't forget my little sister
I told you what to get her.

Love from Ben, age 5.